Mortal Discipline

Phillip Ahn M.D.

NOTE

The initials, "M.D." stand for "Medical Doctor." In the case of Dr. Phillip Ahn, these letters can also stand for many other aspects of his life: Multi-Dimensional, Motivator and Disciplinarian, Mentor and Disciple, Missionary to Developing countries, Multilingual Devotion, Music and Dance, Mindful Dad, and possibly more. Dr. Ahn could be considered a "jack of many trades and a master of a few." As a follow up to his book "Mortal Doctor," Phillip decided to write shorter books on the other aspects of his life mentioned above.

INTRODUCTION

"Whoever loves discipline loves knowledge, but whoever
hates correction is stupid." ~ Proverbs 12:1.

"Whoever disregards discipline comes to poverty and shame, but
whoever heeds correction is honored." ~Proverbs 13:18.

Motivation and discipline were not always character traits of mine when I was a child. Even though I grew up learning and even teaching taekwondo, I was naturally a shy and insecure boy, especially after I immigrated from South Korea to the United States of America at eight years of age. Nevertheless, the tenets of taekwondo that I learned and eventually followed have allowed me to slowly "morph" into a very motivated and disciplined adult. I will share some practical advice for people seeking to do the same, to make the most of their God given talents and opportunities.

THE TENETS OF TAEKWONDO

The five tenets of taekwondo are: **courtesy, integrity, perseverance, self-control and indomitable spirit.** Motivation and discipline encapsulate all of these tenets. It takes self discipline to be courteous to unruly colleagues, patients or strangers. Likewise it takes both motivation and discipline to become a person of integrity, whom others can turn to and count on. Perseverance and indomitable spirit are impossible if one is not motivated and disciplined to patiently suffer through hard work. Self-control and discipline are almost synonymous.

My father, who was also my taekwondo instructor and grandmaster of his very successful schools, became a pastor later in life, when I was in college. Because I grew up with Christian and Biblical principles, the tenets of taekwondo were not foreign concepts to me; these tenets are very much in line with Christian principles. Nevertheless, I struggled to display these character traits until I was in college, starting at age 18. I will share both my struggles and my success stories with my readers.

COURTESY

This tenet of taekwondo is a very necessary aspect of a well-functioning society. Courtesy encompasses other characteristics like respect, especially respect for authority and people who are older and wiser than yourself. In martial arts schools, students and teachers show courtesy by bowing to each other. Students learn courtesy at a young age and are instructed to display this to opponents, as well as teammates and friends.

Children can apply the tenet of courtesy at home by honoring and obeying their parents. This happens to be the fifth of The Ten Commandments that are mentioned in the Bible and displayed in judicial court rooms throughout the United States. The Bible verse in Exodus 20:12 reads, "Honor your father and mother...that your days may be long, and that it may go well with you." The principle of this commandment makes absolute sense and is very practical. Parents are not infallible and are going to make mistakes, but children should still treat them with respect rather than with temper tantrums or insubordination.

I spent my first eight years of life in South Korea. In Korea, I learned that respect for authority and elders is an unspoken rule that is followed by everyone. The Korean language distinguishes between formal and informal tenses of verbs, and one is always expected to use the formal tense when addressing people in authority, in higher standing at work or people who are older than you. If someone deviates from such courteous behavior, that person is shamed or chastised by others, even strangers.

Students in Korea do not dare talk back to or challenge their teachers or coaches, especially in front of other students, teachers, administrators or coaches. Even though I left Korea at eight years of age, I have maintained this respect for authority and the elderly. I always speak to them with courtesy and respect. I also refer to them by their titles rather than their first names. For example, I refer to physicians who are older than me as doctors, and to in-laws as mother, father, grandfather, etc.; I don't call them by their first names. Likewise, I have never called coaches or teachers by their first names and have not allowed my students to call me by my first name.

When I was growing up, I feared my father, who was a strict disciplinarian. I did not always agree with him but almost always honored and obeyed him. Like most kids, I would rather have been playing with my friends after school than doing my homework, practicing piano or even attending taekwondo classes. I was afraid to disobey my parents, especially my dad. So, I usually went along with their wishes and did what I was told. This kept me out of trouble.

Even though my family immigrated to the U.S.when I was eight years old, my parents maintained many Korean traditions, including corporal punishment for misbehavior or insubordination. In my first book I gave an example of this: I stuck out my hands to receive lashings with a stick from my teacher, for not completing my homework.

I was the oldest of four children, so I always received the brunt of the punishment from my father. Even though the manner that the punishment was carried out was organized and never abusive, I still hated it as a child, as you can imagine. Nevertheless, the punishment I received curbed my behavior and kept me on the straight and narrow.

As I grew up to become a disciplined and hard working adult, I realized that the lessons from my parents helped mold me into a man who lives by principles rather than fleeting desires. When I started to study to become a physician, I learned to sacrifice my desire to watch TV, play sports or just hang out with friends, in order to achieve my academic goals. Listening to my parents and respecting other people of authority helped me to mature into the man I am today. I have in turn taught and passed on this tenet of courtesy to my daughter, taekwondo students, patients, friends and even strangers.

Students of all ages need to display courtesy in school, towards teachers, administrators, counselors and fellow students. Realize that people in authority almost always have good intentions and have a common goal to see you succeed. These people of authority should treat you with respect as well, but as a student you should learn to swallow your pride and be patient, regardless of their methods. Instead of reacting negatively, which can result in long term consequences, learn to be courteous in all situations.

The most successful athletes are labeled as "coachable" because they realize that coaches want to bring out the best in their athletes and take pride in seeing them succeed. These athletes are usually great team players as well, looking out for the best interest of everyone. Such behavior is the quintessential example of courtesy.

When I played team sports, I did not always agree with my coaches' decisions, especially if they placed me in positions or a part of the lineup that I did not like. Even though I was quiet and shy by nature, I was a gifted and competitive athlete, and I wanted to be the star on all of my teams. When coaches put me in situations that did not allow this to happen, I bit my lip, held my tongue and "took one for the team."

Scottie Pippen is a hall of fame NBA basketball player who was Michael Jordan's sidekick on the Chicago Bulls team that is regarded as the best basketball team of all time, winning six championships. He has one huge blemish on his NBA resume, however. Jordan had retired for the first time before the 1994 season began, and Pippen was considered to be the new star of the Bulls. During a playoff game that season, the Bulls were tied against the New York Knicks with 1.8 seconds left. Coach Phil Jackson called a time out and designed a play that involved Pippen passing the ball to Toni Kukoc for the last shot. Scottie did not agree with this decision and refused to return to the court. This forced Jackson to substitute another player for Pippen who did throw the ball to Kukoc, who then made the game winning shot. The TV cameras turned to Pippen, who looked like a self-centered diva that made an incredibly regrettable decision.

△△△

I am a physician and I definitely believe that ADHD (attention deficit and hyperactivity disorder) and ODD (oppositional defiant disorder) are legitimate diagnoses. Nevertheless, I also believe that if children learned and followed the taekwondo tenet of courtesy, there would be less children diagnosed with these disorders. Parenting is not easy, but parents must try, both verbally and by example, to guide their children to display appropriate behavior in all situations. Courtesy must be encouraged and exemplified in the academic, athletic and social arenas. Children who learn this and incorporate these behaviors early in life will continue to do so as they become hard working adults. In contrast, those who do not learn the concept of courtesy may become juvenile delinquents or sociopaths.

It takes motivation and discipline to display courtesy in many real life situations. Courtesy can easily be displayed by opening the door for other people or giving up your seat on the bus to an elderly person. On the other hand, one must be very motivated to be courteous to those who disagree with you, are unnecessarily demanding, or display other rude and inconsiderate behavior. It takes discipline to walk away from a fight or argument, swallow your pride, and "be the bigger man." Of course, these cliches hold true for women as well.

I have experienced the following discourteous acts throughout my lifetime, and they have become my pet peeves:

I cannot understand why people double park on the street, in alleys and even in front of other people's garages, making it difficult or even impossible to get out of one's parking spot or garage. My frustration gets worse when I confront these rude drivers about their inconsiderate actions and instead of apologizing, they swear at me or just act like it is their right to inconvenience me. Please be aware and considerate when you look for a parking spot, and apologize if your actions cause others difficulty getting out of their parking spot or garage.

I am also bewildered by inconsiderate drivers who get into the passing lane, which is usually the left hand lane, and then drive slower than the others. Some of these drivers will also honk their horns, shine their headlights at you or even "flip you the bird" if you pass them, instead of realizing that they are violating a basic tenet of driving, "slower traffic keep right." The same principle applies to pedestrians who take up entire sidewalks or bike paths and act indignant when you ask them to move to the right to pass them. Please be considerate and leave plenty of room for people to pass you.

Pedestrians can also be inconsiderate to drivers and not merely to fellow pedestrians. It is beyond logical reasoning why some people think that it is their right to cross the street when the traffic signal for the cars, not the pedestrians, turns green. I also can't understand such discourteous behavior when people take their time crossing to the other side, in the middle of the street (i.e., not using the crosswalk), and even become indignant or swear at drivers while doing so. Please, show courtesy and try not to be self-centered.

△△△

Martial arts students are taught to be good sports (gracious winners and not sore losers) no matter the outcome of a match. Obedience and honoring your coaches are ingrained into all students. Coaches in turn are expected to display courtesy to referees and other judges, as well as their students, opponents and opposing coaches.

Unfortunately, there are several examples of martial artists and instructors who do not display this basic martial arts tenet. The Kobra Kai clan in The Karate Kid movies is a classic example. The students and the sensei from this school were bullies who constantly picked on weaker people, including Daniel ("Daniel-san") LaRusso. They had to learn a hard lesson about courtesy from Mr. Miyagi and his student Daniel-san, who ultimately got the best of these bullies by beating them at an annual tournament that they had previously dominated.

I have not always swallowed my pride and walked away from arguments or fights. As martial artists, we are taught to only resort to violence in situations of self-defense or defending another person. I can proudly say that I have not physically fought anyone since graduating from high school. Even the last physical fight in which I was involved was somewhat of a good example.

I was playing in a pickup football game in high school but suffered a knee injury at the beginning of the game, so I watched from the sidelines. In the middle of the game I noticed a scuffle, so I limped my way over to check it out. An opposing player was fighting with one of my teammates. By the time I arrived on the scene, the fight had broken up and the combatants were about to shake hands. Instead of shaking hands, however, my opponent sucker punched my teammate in the face and he fell to the ground. Everyone was in shock but nobody intervened, so I hit the perpetrator and knocked him to the ground. This resulted in a huge melee involving both teams. Eventually order was restored, no one suffered any serious physical consequences and no legal action was taken.

Displaying courtesy is not always easy and I will admit that I have failed many times. Even though I have not physically fought anyone since becoming an adult, I have been guilty of the following discourteous reactions: retaliating when a driver intentionally cut me off - I have blasted my horn or shone the high beam lights at such drivers; returning hateful speech when someone made fun of me or swore at me; arguing loudly to clearly state my point of view, even to friends and family.

Such displays of discourteous behavior have resulted in some strained relationships with my family, friends and coworkers. Even though I am a chief villain in a popular video game, I am not proud of any of my actions in real life when I have not displayed courtesy. While none of my actions have resulted in any legal consequences, the guilty feelings that sometimes sneak into my memory are not pleasant, and I long to apologize for my actions to anyone that I have wronged. I do try to "live and learn," and live without regrets, as I stated in my first book, "Mortal Doctor."

I can honestly say that I have taken the tenet of courtesy to heart. People who know me today would definitely describe me as a courteous person. I try my hardest to be considerate to others, sacrifice my needs for the needs of those around me and demonstrate the life of a gentleman.

I am very grateful for my Christian upbringing that has ingrained in me the principle of treating others as I would want to be treated. I encourage all of my readers to follow this golden rule and to follow the tenet of taekwondo, courtesy. Try to look beyond your own needs and desires and see what you can do for those around you, especially the physically or emotionally hurting.

Here are some ways you can show courtesy: open doors for others; don't eat before other guests; give up your seat on a bus or train for an elderly or pregnant person; consider the potential inconvenience you are causing others when you park your car; stay in the right (slow) lane while driving, on the bike path or sidewalk and let others easily pass you; ask how others (friends, family, strangers you meet) are doing; seek out opportunities to serve rather than be served; don't look down or make fun of others but try to help them; show respect to everyone, especially those in authority and your elders.

SELF-REFLECTION:

Who do you know that models courteous behavior?

What can you do to display courtesy today at home,
school, work place, or in the public arena?

What habits can you develop to remind yourself to be more courteous?

INTEGRITY

Honesty, integrity, reliability and responsibility are all branches from the same tree. One must be very motivated and disciplined to become someone of high integrity, which equates to a person of upstanding character. Yes, I am a bad character in Mortal Kombat 2, but in real life I am a physician and father who tries to be a person who is responsible and reliable. I try to be someone that my friends, family members and even strangers can turn to when they need help.

People need help in several ways: physically, emotionally, financially and spiritually. As a physician, I abide by the Hippocratic Oath to treat my patients to the best of my ability for their best outcomes. I have to display integrity with each of my patients, regardless of their social situation, whether they are sinners or saints. This sometimes means that I go against their preconceived ideas or agenda. Examples include: not prescribing antibiotics for viral illnesses, narcotics for addicted patients, unnecessary tests for anxious patients or those with Munchausen syndrome, and blindly refilling medications to patients with chronic illnesses who have not seen a physician for a long time.

In general I have good rapport with my patients and they show great respect, trust and loyalty towards me. I have some patients who have gotten angry with me because they did not get their way and have even threatened to sue me. In these situations I have apologized if I was wrong, stood firmly with my decisions if I did what I thought was right, and fired some patients from my practice if they continued to display non-compliant or disrespectful behavior towards my staff or myself. I have never been a defendant in a malpractice suit.

ΔΔΔ

Fatherhood involves daily displays of integrity. A father must do what is best for his son or daughter, and not necessarily give into his child's desires. If a child throws temper tantrums because he or she cannot have a new toy, eat junk food or watch hours of television, the easy thing for a parent to do would be to give in, to appease the child. Instead of giving in to your child, you should find an alternative activity or healthy food that the child will still enjoy, and when the child has calmed down, you can gently explain the rationale for your actions. It takes motivation to lovingly discipline your child for their wellbeing, long term development and success.

As soon as my daughter was born, I was determined to be a "loving disciplinarian." Such a title involves providing gentle guidance, standing firm when necessary and following through on your word when children misbehave, instead of making empty promises or threats. Too many of my patients' parents threaten punishment to their children when they misbehave, even in my office, and never follow through. These same parents then wonder why their children misbehave and get reprimanded in school when they are older.

Children should be taught the concept of integrity as early in life as possible. When toddlers get caught doing something that they think will get them in trouble, some will tell a fib. Most parents can easily decipher these acts of deception. These situations serve as great opportunities for parents to ingrain into these impressionable minds that honesty is the best policy. Parents should teach their children that people who lie have to tell another lie to cover up the first one, that it's impossible to keep their stories consistent, and that it's clearly wrong to lie.

Learning to admit one's fault or wrongdoing and owning up to their responsibility is also a valuable lesson that children can carry into adulthood. Parents are not perfect. Admitting when you are wrong or don't have all the answers is a part of parental integrity. A child will grow to become a reliable and responsible adult if he or she witnesses good modeling. These early childhood lessons will create men and women who will make great leaders, employees and model citizens. In contrast, a child will grow to be someone who never follows through on their responsibilities or promises, if they think such behavior is normal. I'm amazed at how many people fit into the latter category, resulting in dropping out of school(s), going from job to job, and always struggling to survive.

Throughout my life as a father, especially after my ex-wife asked for a separation and eventual divorce, I noticed that my daughter valued trust and integrity above all other character traits. With God's help, I have indeed been faithful in keeping my promises to my daughter. She has expressed to me over and over that I am her hero and role model, and that she intends to follow in my footsteps and become a physician.

△△△

When you hear of acts of heroism and integrity in the news, you see the following examples. Someone finds a large amount of money, a wallet or purse or other valuables, and turns it into the proper authorities, not expecting a reward. A football player finds an opposing team's playbook and turns it into his coach. They both call the opposing team's coach to inform him of this, before their game. A student finds the answers to an upcoming exam in a classroom as he is leaving. He turns it into his teacher or principal instead of keeping it or trying to sell it to his classmates.

In the workplace, a man or woman who has a reputation for integrity will be seen as reliable and be given more and more responsibility, which usually results in promotions and successful careers. Yes, there are examples of leaders, especially in politics, who have obtained their positions via corruption rather than legitimate means. These crooked people usually suffer severe consequences in the form of bad reputations, financial loss, strained relationships with friends and family, or even jail time. On rare occasions, someone may leave their job or their career to stand up for their integrity.

When I was in high school, I received mostly A's in math classes. In one math class, I sat next to a student who later went into Chicago politics. At the end of the school year, I took my final exam one day before she would take the same exam. She asked me to jot down my answers on a piece of paper and stated that she would pay for this. Even though I did not have much money and both of my parents worked very hard to provide for my family, I did not accept this offer. I remembered my father's lessons on Christian values and his taekwondo lessons about integrity.

SELF-REFLECTION:

Can you describe a moment in your life when you or someone else displayed integrity?

What can you do today at home, at work or school, or even to strangers
you meet to demonstrate this character?

PERSEVERANCE

" And let us run with perseverance the race marked out for us…" ~ Hebrew 12:1.

To persevere means to not give up or give in to stressful situations or obstacles that get in your way of achieving a goal. Life is full of challenges but also full of successful examples of perseverance: a mother enduring a difficult pregnancy and painful labor but giving birth to the joy of her life; an athlete exercising daily and rehabbing after injury until achieving the goal of becoming a champion in their sport; a martial artist practicing techniques every day until obtaining a black belt; a detective working on a cold case until finally solving a murder mystery; a college student studying more and more difficult classes until obtaining his or her medical degree; someone suffering through physical or emotional challenges in life but holding onto their faith in God.

Those who persevere through trials and tribulations that they experience go the furthest in life, while those who give up along the way or just coast along because they are handed everything on a silver platter fall short of maximizing their potential. One must usually suffer through and trudge along in life to make the most of their God given talents and opportunities.

Parents can teach perseverance to their children at an early age. They can complete puzzles together, assemble intricate toys or games, have children assist in household chores and projects, and make sure that they complete all of their homework and school projects, always giving their best effort.

Children are often thrust into many activities, starting at a young age. These include baseball, soccer, gymnastics, music, dance and martial arts. These are very healthy activities that can lead to healthy kids with great self esteem. All of these activities, however, can have their ups and downs. No one can win all of their matches or always be the best on their team or always give perfect recitals. Parents and coaches should teach their children that it is indeed not whether you win or lose, but that what matters most is the lessons you learn along the way. Children can apply these lessons to other aspects of their lives such as schoolwork and personal relationships, and in the workforce when they are adults.

I placed my daughter into many activities when she was growing up, starting with swimming lessons when she was barely able to walk. She also dabbled in gymnastics, taekwondo (in which she earned her first degree black belt), and other sports, before she started to concentrate on tennis and volleyball. She certainly experienced her share of "the thrill of victory and the agony of defeat." Throughout the process, she has learned the value of hard work and preparation, as well as lessons in integrity and fair play, while learning to persevere through the bad times and cherish the good times. These lessons have culminated in her being recruited to play college tennis, after having an incredible high school career in both tennis and volleyball.

Great coaches are often referred to as father figures by superstar athletes. This is because these coaches bring out the best in their players in life, not just in their particular sport. Teaching perseverance to athletes, especially young ones, is one of the best life lessons that parents can give their children. Teach them to always give their best effort, be a gracious winner and not a sore loser, and only give up their sport or other activity when it is clear that their talents have been exhausted and they should no longer pursue that particular activity.

When I was in junior high school, I was forced to take piano lessons by my parents. I liked the idea of being a great pianist, but I did not like to practice, so I did not master this skill. I prematurely quit lessons after a couple of years. I did the same with guitar lessons in high school. I would absolutely love to be able to play both of these instruments proficiently. These are examples of lack of perseverance on my part.

When I was in high school, I played for my school's baseball, ice hockey and gymnastics teams, each for one year or less. I was a naturally gifted athlete in terms of strength, speed, jumping ability and hand-eye coordination. I was already a black belt in taekwondo. I did not apply the discipline I learned in taekwondo to other areas of my life, however. I did not like to train hard at something unless it was fun or easy for me. If there was a player ahead of me or better than me at a sport or position, I gave up, instead of working harder than that person or trying to improve myself.

I am happy to say that everything changed in college. I agreed with my father to study pre-medicine because being a physician sounded like a noble career. Deep inside, I did not think that I was smart enough or disciplined enough to get into medical school. Nevertheless, because I agreed with my father, I became determined to give my best effort in college. If I didn't get into medical school, I could honestly admit that I gave my best shot.

God completely changed ("morphed") me in college. I went from not studying in high school to studying all the time, even during vacations. I did not give up when I took difficult classes like Organic Chemistry, which is the class that makes or breaks many pre-med students. I persevered and was accepted into the University of Illinois College of Medicine, my first choice of medical schools.

Developing perseverance in academics also "morphed" me to become a better athlete, albeit at recreational and intramural levels. I have been a starter or captain on several championship football and volleyball teams, and have played through too many injuries to count. While persevering in my athletic endeavors, I have learned to balance my work, family and social life. I have passed on my lessons in perseverance to my daughter, and this has resulted in her becoming an all-state tennis and volleyball player while also being her high school's valedictorian and homecoming queen. She has done this in spite of her mother separating from and eventually divorcing me when my daughter was 10 years old.

My daughter is currently playing college tennis while studying pre-medicine. She has been on many mission trips to developing countries, and has accompanied me on a few occasions. I am confident that she will become a great physician, not merely like her dad, but greater than him!

Shortly after I separated from my ex-wife, I attended a salsa party. Before attending this event, I had considered myself to be a good dancer who would even "start the party" at wedding receptions and similar gatherings. Trying to dance salsa, however, was incredibly challenging and made my insecure personality reemerge. I hated the feeling of not being good at this skill and could decipher from my partners' faces that they knew I didn't know how to dance. It took me almost three months, but I swallowed my pride and started taking salsa lessons. I practiced it as much as my free time allowed, and pretty soon became proficient. Many of the same women from that first salsa party I attended told me that I was the quickest learner that they had ever seen.

Learning to dance salsa allowed me to pick up other types of dances, even without taking lessons, and allowed me to develop an ear for music that I did not pick up after I quit piano and guitar lessons as a teenager. These days I am often asked if I am a dance instructor or on a dance performance team, for which I am flattered. Even though I learned to dance formally when I was in my late 40s, I did not let my initial insecurities and sense of rejection stop me from pursuing my goals of mastering this skill.

ΔΔΔ

As I mentioned earlier, I was not a motivated student until I developed a goal of getting into medical school, when I started my undergraduate studies. I have met other physicians who were even later bloomers. Some of these doctors were not even accepted into medical schools in the United States and had to pay a lot of money to attend schools in foreign countries, mostly in the caribbean islands. Once they arrived at their destinations, these desperate students buckled down, studied to pass their classes and board exams, and successfully matched into residency programs in the U.S.

These late bloomers eventually became successful attending physicians. These physicians demonstrated perseverance in that while achieving their goal was not easy, they did not lose sight of their destination. They continued to work and work until they finally made it count.

A famous example of perseverance is that of Elizabeth Smart. When she was 14 years old, she was kidnapped, raped and held captive by Brian Mitchell and his wife. Even though she was so young and suffered what no woman should at any age, she persevered in her will to live and return to normalcy. She was finally rescued after nine months. After she was reunited with her family, she gave many interviews, wrote a memoir, became a child safety activist and journalist, and eventually got married and had children.

Perseverance can definitely be displayed through your faith and belief system. In my first book I wrote that I am a Calvinist Christian and believe in the acronym TULIP. The P stands for Perseverance of the Saints. This means that once you become a child of God, it's impossible to leave His family. True Christians should and will keep the faith no matter what trials and tribulations they face in life.

> "I have fought the good fight, I have endured the race,
> I have kept the faith." ~ 2 Timothy 4:7.

The apostle Paul wrote this when he was imprisoned in Rome for his Christian faith.

SELF-REFLECTION:

Do you know someone who has persevered through great tribulations?

Are you someone who gives up easily or do you persevere
until your tasks are completed?

What can you do today that you have not finished or have given
up on, to develop and demonstrate perseverance?

SELF-CONTROL

"The fruit of the Spirit is love, joy, peace, patience, kindness, goodness, faithfulness, gentleness and self-control."   ~Galatians 5:22 - 23.

Christians are called to display certain characteristics, known as the fruit of the Holy Spirit. The only tenet of taekwondo that is also a fruit of the Spirit is self-control. It is synonymous with self-discipline. Everyone needs to use self-control every day in some way, both in small and not so small matters. As Peter Parker was told when he became Spiderman, "With great power comes great responsibility." To be a responsible person, one needs great self-control.

Parenting involves an incredible amount of self-control. Babies require all of their parents' attention to stay alive: be fed, have diapers changed, sung lullabies to sleep, and in general be comforted and feel loved. Patience is a part of self-control and is vital for parents, especially young or first time parents. Unfortunately, there are too many news reports of parents who lose self-control and severely harm or kill their babies by shaking them, hitting them or neglecting them.

As babies become toddlers and young children, parents not only need to exercise self-control themselves, but they need to teach their children the same. Through loving discipline, parents must teach their children how to develop self-control and appropriate coping mechanisms instead of throwing temper tantrums, hitting other people or otherwise displaying bratty and inappropriate behavior. Teaching and modeling self-control and appropriate reactions to stressful or undesirable situations are critical to the development of children when they start interacting with peers, teachers, coaches and other figures of authority as they grow and mature into adults.

Even though my daughter was a very easy baby and toddler who did not require much correction, she definitely tested my patience at times. By being a loving disciplinarian and by being involved in all aspects of her life - feeding, changing diapers, teaching her sports and helping her academically, I established and maintained a solid bond with her and built a foundation for her to succeed in future endeavors.

As I have previously mentioned, I believe that ADHD and ODD are legitimate medical diagnoses. I also mentioned, and will re-emphasize, that if children are taught the concept of self-control by their parents, many less children would be given these diagnoses. More children would learn how to manage their symptoms and handle stressful situations with healthy and appropriate responses.

Self-control also involves the handling of pets and other animals. Teaching a pet self-control can be very challenging, but it can lead to a fulfilling, life long bond. On the other hand, cruelty to animals is an early sign of conduct disorder. Children who display such behavior may later develop into adolescents or adults with psychopathic or antisocial personality disorder. Please learn proper methods to care for and train your pets and pass these lessons onto children.

△△△

The United States and many other parts of the world have an epidemic of obesity. This phenomenon results in severe consequences for children, including type 2 or adult-onset diabetes. The youngest of my patients given this diagnosis was an eight years old girl.

While there definitely is a genetic component to obesity, the lack of self-control is largely responsible for this epidemic. Parents are not teaching or modeling self-control when it comes to nutrition, in terms of healthy choices of food and proper portions. The same holds true for exercise, or more accurately, the lack of exercise. Self-control means learning and consuming what is beneficial for your body's overall health, not eating to satisfy boredom or to try to relieve stress.

People who exercise self-control know when they are satisfied, have eaten enough, and do not "pig out" because there is still food at the table or in the refrigerator that will give them immediate gratification. Those who lack self-control of their eating become addicted to food's effects, exactly in the same way drug addicts get addicted to the immediate and very temporary pleasure of narcotics.

As I mentioned in my first book, I do not advocate any extreme diets or even the latest exercise craze, that one cannot maintain for the rest of his or her life. What I do advocate and prescribe to my patients is "vitamin D," D for discipline. I also prescribe "vitamin E," E for exercise and "vitamin B", B for Balance. Discipline and balance are the keys when it comes to diet and exercise.

Speaking of exercise, involvement in sports involves great amounts of self-control. Athletes need discipline to work hard to improve their skills and develop fine-tuned bodies. Even if you are naturally strong, fast or otherwise talented in a particular sport, your competition will pass you up if you don't exercise discipline and continue to work hard. The best athletes in any particular sport are also the hardest workers. The best example of a hard worker is Michael Jordan, who won six NBA championships with the Chicago Bulls and is considered the best basketball player ever, if not the greatest overall athlete of all time.

Athletes must also exercise self-control during matches. While some athletes play their best when they are motivated by anger or even hatred towards their opponents, most athletes who lose self-control and lose their temper commit actions that result in penalties and technical fouls that sometimes result in the loss of major matches.

Serena Williams is one of the greatest tennis players of all time, but she lost her temper after some questionable calls by the chair umpire during the 2018 U.S. Open finals and subsequently lost the match. She was fined $17,000 for her unprofessional behavior. Sometimes such displays of lacking self-control taint what is otherwise a legendary career.

Novak Djokovic, one of the greatest male tennis players of all time, was once fined a greater amount, $267,500. He lost his temper and angrily hit a tennis ball that recklessly injured a line judge during the 2020 U.S. Open. He was also disqualified from his fourth round match and the rest of the tournament.

There's a saying in sports that you always get caught (by referees) when you retaliate. Some "agitators" take advantage of this and try to get under the skin of opponents to draw a penalty. Examples of agitators include Esa Tikkanen and Sean Avery of the NHL and too many "trash talkers" in the NBA and NFL to mention. Self-control and trusting that these people will get their just due is recommended, and this usually yields the best results. This advice holds true for players, coaches and managers.

I really admire cool and collected coaches who motivate and bring out the best out of their players through sound guidance and principles, not by being loud tyrants who throw temper tantrums, cuss out their players and referees or dish out unreasonable punishment. Tom Landry of the Dallas Cowboys and Tom Osborne of the Nebraska Cornhuskers are two classic examples of cool and composed coaches.

Exercising self-control and not retaliating pertains to all aspects of life. Some scenarios when self-restraint rather than retaliation is prudent include: getting cut off in traffic, being the butt of jokes or insults, being discriminated against or racially profiled. I have definitely experienced all of these wrongdoings by other people throughout my life.

When I was a child, after I immigrated from Korea to Chicago, I sometimes retaliated physically against bullies and other kids who taunted me for being Asian. Even though I was never the initiator of the bullying and racial taunting, I wish that I had demonstrated more self control against these perpetrators. I can proudly say that I have not resorted to this tactic since I have become an adult.

I have played in a couple of flag football leagues during my free time as a physician. Some of my opponents, most of whom were middle aged men, taunted, hurled profanity and needlessly tried to get under my skin. I wanted to give them a taste of their own medicine, but I swallowed my pride and tried to beat them by playing better than them.

On one occasion, in a co-ed football league championship game, a petite female receiver caught a pass and was about to score a touchdown. I ran as fast as I could, caught up to her and reached out for her flag. In doing so, I grabbed some of her clothing and dragged her down to the ground. When we were both on the ground, she kicked me and some of her players came over and pushed me (albeit not hard). I could easily have physically retaliated and kicked my opponents, which probably would have started a riot and given me a criminal record for battery.

Instead of retaliating, I exercised self-control and reasoned with my opponents, stating that it was an accident and that if I had intentionally tackled the receiver, she would have been seriously hurt. This resulted in all of us shaking hands and both teams finishing the game without any negative and permanent consequences. "See the big picture" and show self-control in all situations.

Seeing the big picture also came into play one day shortly after the infamous day of terror in U.S. history known as "9-11." I led a group of students and young adults to a park to play pick up football after church. As we were heading to the field, we heard a group of young men hurling ethnic slurs at us because we were Asians, even though they themselves belonged to a minority group. This brought back childhood memories when I physically fought with kids who taunted me.

Instead of returning hateful speech or getting into a fight with these young men, I challenged them to a game of football. They gladly accepted our challenge and appeared very cocky, thinking that they would beat us. Their quarterback was the cockiest and loudest player. I was the quarterback of my team.

We scored a touchdown during every one of our ball possessions and intercepted their pass each time they had the ball. Within fifteen minutes we were winning 35 - 0, so their quarterback said, "We give up. You guys are good." Hopefully, he and the rest of his team learned a valuable lesson in humility.

Self-control and controlling your temper is even more critical when it involves other, more serious aspects of life. The topic I am bringing up here is domestic violence. This is another epidemic that needs to be curbed, in a major way. While corporal punishment is accepted in some cultures, it is usually carried out in an organized, systematic way that is understood by students or military recruits as consequences for misbehavior or insubordination. Violence that is a result of a loss of temper, especially when the victim is a child or spouse who weighs much less than the perpetrator and cannot easily defend him or herself, is absolutely wrong. Men and women, you are not macho or brave if you resort to hitting weaker people, especially those you say you love.

Several studies have demonstrated that children have lower intelligence quotas and poor development if they are abused or if they grow up in a home where their parents fight in front of them. This is part of what's called "Toxic Stress Syndrome," which can have severe consequences like depression (including suicide), conduct disorder and a life of crime. These children repeat the cycle of abuse when they become adults, unless they receive proper counseling and treatment.

Parents need to recognize the stress that their children may be experiencing, especially from the actions of their parents. As I mentioned in my first book, LOVE = TIME, both in terms of quality and quantity. Parents need to be involved in the activities of their children, guide them with loving discipline and set good examples of appropriate behavior. These actions will be key contributors to relieving the toxic stress syndrome.

Domestic violence is more common if one also does not show self-control over alcohol, or if one abuses narcotics or other addictive substances. In my first book I told my story of the lessons about alcohol that I learned as a teenager and how I promised God that I would never become drunk again. While being accepted by friends and co-workers may be important for your self-esteem, showing self-control by drinking in moderation (usually 1 - 2 drinks per day) and abstaining from addictive substances usually results in admiration from your peers. I implore my readers to examine their drinking and other unhealthy habits and to exercise self-control over their own bodies.

SELF-REFLECTION:

Who in your life has modeled great self-control?

What areas in your life show a lack of self-control?

What steps can you take today to start working on these areas?

INDOMITABLE SPIRIT

The legendary football coach Vince Lombardi stated, "Winning is not everything; it's the only thing." Indomitable spirit *can* be interpreted as "winning at all costs." As a taekwondo tenet, however, the meaning of indomitable spirit is more accurately defined by another famous coach, Jim Valvano, who said, "Never give up. Don't ever give up." He was dying from cancer when he said this.

Children who are taught this principle learn not to give up when the going gets tough, which is inevitable in life. This holds true for academics, athletics, and even relationships. This can also hold true for not letting physical limitations like congenital deformities or major injuries hold them back from pursuing their goals and dreams.

Bethany Hamilton grew up surfing in Kauai, Hawaii. When she was only 13 years old, a tiger shark bit off her left arm while she was on her surfboard. Instead of thinking that she would never surf again, she rehabilitated quickly and resumed surfing only one month after the shark attack. She subsequently enjoyed a prolific career as a professional surfer, as well as a motivational speaker and author. Her life is chronicled in the popular movie, Soul Surfer.

Some of the greatest athletes of all time are quarterbacks like Tom Brady and Aaron Rodgers. No matter how much of a deficit that their team has or how little time is left in the game, these leaders consistently rally their teams to victories, including Super Bowls. They not only display indomitable spirit but also instill this into their teammates. The best example of this is the 2017 Super Bowl. The Atlanta Falcons looked dominant and took a 28 - 3 over the New England Patriots. Instead of giving up, Tom Brady led the Patriots to beat the Falcons 34 - 28, marking the biggest comeback in Super Bowl history.

I remember watching Serena Williams, possibly the greatest female tennis player of all time, playing in the 2014 Beijing, China Open. She was trailing in one match 0 - 5 in the first set and her opponent had set point. I am glad that I did not turn the television off. I witnessed an incredible display of indomitable spirit, as Serena rallied to win the set 7 -5 and subsequently win the match 7 -5, 6 - 2. Williams later revealed that she was a little sick, but that she did not want to "get bageled," which is a tennis term for losing 0 - 6. She just kept fighting one point at a time, displayed more indomitable spirit than her opponent and eventually defeated her.

I am also glad that I witnessed one of the greatest upsets in boxing history, involving a previously little known boxer named James "Buster" Douglas. He was the challenger against one of the greatest heavyweights of all time, Mike Tyson. Tyson had destroyed all of his opponents, usually by knocking them out in the first round. The TV announcer even commented that it was a miracle when Buster survived the first round. Instead of giving into pressure and expectations, Buster went on to win the match, by knocking Mike Tyson out! Buster accomplished this in spite being knocked down earlier in the match. Douglas was "down but not out," and he definitely demonstrated indomitable spirit.

The greatest athletes also display indomitable spirit by playing through injuries, for the sake of the team. Some professional athletes have played with broken bones, respiratory infections and even appendicitis. Patrick Roy, one of the greatest goalies in NHL history, refused to have surgery for his appendicitis because he did not want to miss the 1994 playoffs. He chose to receive intravenous antibiotics and postponed surgery until his team was eventually eliminated from the playoffs.

Michael Jordan, possibly the greatest professional athlete in any sport, won the 1997 NBA championship with the Chicago Bulls while playing with a 102 degree fever in Game 5. The following year, his teammate Scottie Pippen played Game 6 of the NBA finals with severe back pain. He acted as a decoy, while his teammates played bigger roles than usual. Michael Jordan had to burden most of the load. MJ's come from behind game winning shot to end that game, which secured his sixth and last championship, has become an iconic sports highlight.

I have also played through many injuries, albeit not in such important situations as those mentioned. When I was already over 40 years of age, I played in a two game flag football tournament. On one play I went to grab the flag of an opponent when I felt sudden sharp pain in my right pinkie (fifth finger). I noticed that the tip of my finger had dislocated after I ran into my opponent, so I pulled it back into place and finished the game.

After the game, I noticed that the finger remained deformed because the tendon had ruptured. We won the game, so the next day I taped my finger to keep it functional, and we won the championship. To this day you can see that this finger, along with many of my other fingers, have suffered many traumatic sports injuries.

Even though I am citing these extraordinary acts of courage and indomitable spirit in these athletes, I am not, by any means, proposing that recreational athletes should do the same. Keep the proper perspective of what is most important in your life. Don't jeopardize your job or home life in pursuit of playing or even winning recreational sports matches. In other words, "Kids, don't try this at home!"

There are many movies that demonstrate indomitable spirit: Die Hard, Rudy, Rocky, The Karate Kid, Bloodsport and most other martial arts movies. For those that are not familiar with these movies, here is a brief synopsis of each.

In Die Hard, John McLane, a New York cop who happened to be visiting his estranged wife at her work Christmas party in Los Angeles, fought against all odds in defeating an international terrorist group all by himself. Rudy, whose real name is Daniel Ruettiger, was an average high school football player whose dream was to play for the prestigious Notre Dame Fighting Irish football team. He practiced hard, never gave up and eventually earned some playing time by garnering the admiration of his teammates and fans. Rocky never gives up no matter who his opponent is or how many times he gets knocked down in all of his boxing matches.

Daniel-san, the Karate Kid, overcomes incredible odds as well as a crippling injury to defeat his heavily favored opponents, who were his bullies in everyday life. Frank Dux, played by Jean Claude Van Damme in Bloodsport, defeated the reigning champion, even after the champion cheated by throwing a substance into Dux's eyes to temporarily blind him. Instead of panicking and giving up, Dux remembered his special training that prepared him for such a situation.

Indomitable spirit can even be demonstrated by gamers. Imagine the following scenario: A player (using Shang Tsung as his character, of course) is facing Shao Kahn in the final battle of Mortal Kombat 2. He barely won the first round, but lost the second round by "Flawless Victory." There is much stress and it would be easy for the player to give up. Instead of succumbing to pressure, the player displays indomitable spirit, summons up all of his courage and concentration, and beats Shao Kahn to win the whole tournament!

I started this chapter with a quote from Jimmy Valvano, who eventually succumbed to his cancer. On the other hand, there are many examples of survivors of devastating and even terminal illnesses whose indomitable spirit and "the will to live" kept them alive. These people had their health restored against all odds and against research based expectations from modern medicine.

Indomitable spirit can be displayed all the way up to the point of death. Dying for your faith and principles definitely exemplifies this. In the Bible, the apostles, especially Paul, were never dissuaded from displaying their faith, even when they were imprisoned. Paul and other apostles who became the founding fathers of the Christian faith were persecuted and ultimately killed, but they never recanted their beliefs and principles. Paul states in the Bible that not only are difficulties in life inevitable, but they are opportunities to grow, and even become catalysts for great things to happen. All things work together for the greater good, even in death.

There are modern day examples of martyrs and imprisoned missionaries who do not give up and give in, when they are faced with trials and tribulations. Although I did not personally know him, I went to college with Andrew Brunson, who later served as a missionary in Turkey for many years. He was falsely arrested and imprisoned, but he never wavered in his faith. After nearly two years in a Turkish prison, he won his freedom and was returned to his home country, the United States. He was invited to a press conference at the White House, where he prayed for the president on national television. One of the main concepts that I try to follow is, "Let go and let God." Indomitable spirit can reflect this principle.

"What good is it for a man to gain the whole world but
lose his soul?" ~ Matthew 16:26.

SELF-REFLECTION:

Who do you know that has displayed examples of indomitable spirit?

In what areas of your life do you give up easily and let circumstances defeat you?

What can you do today to start becoming someone who does not
give up and instead displays indomitable spirit?

CONCLUSION

Motivation and Discipline are admirable qualities that may seem unachievable to some of my readers. I know that I struggled with these characteristics early in my life. In this book I have discussed how applying the principles of taekwondo can help you to achieve goals and change your life to start to "morph" into someone who displays these qualities. I can tell you first hand that these are indeed achievable goals for everyone. Start taking small steps in all aspects of your life to become a motivated and disciplined person today!